The Chine

MIMI KHALVATI, born in Tehran in 1944, grew up on the Isle of Wight and attended Drama Centre, London. She co-founded the Theatre in Exile group. She now runs The Poetry School, offering courses and workshops in London. Carcanet publish *In White Ink* (1991), *Mirrorwork* (1995), *Entries on Light* (1998) and *Selected Poems* (2000).

'Mimi Khalvati is a prolific and courageous poet who has produced what for some would be a lifetime's body of work in a short decade. *The Chine*, her fifth book, is a marvel of generosity, which mirrors the contours and contradictions of the poet's history. No question that in Khalvati's work form *is* content, and content form, which is consistent with one of her sources, the Persian language and its literary tradition, as well as with Persian graphic and fabric arts. The fact that the forms she largely chooses are those traditional to European prosody – terza rima, the sonnet, the sestina, various nonce iambic pentameter stanzas – exemplifies another facet of this poet's singularity and paradox.

Her work establishes a dialogue, neither adversarial nor acquiescent, but a peer's give-and-take with the poets of the canon which we must now name "Anglophone" without the parochialism of a nationality. But one doesn't read Mimi Khalvati's poetry for what it represents; one reads it for its music, its sensuality, its irony, its excess, for the way it owns and articulates the tragicomedy of one woman's life (and thus myriad lives) as it spans an ocean, two languages, several cultures, and now two centuries.'

Marilyn Hacker

Also by Mimi Khalvati

In White Ink
Mirrorwork
Entries on Light
Selected Poems

MIMI KHALVATI

The Chine

CARCANET

Published in Great Britain in 2002 by
Carcanet Press Limited
4th Floor, Conavon Court
12–16 Blackfriars Street
Manchester M3 5BQ

A CIP catalogue record for this book
is available from the British Library

ISBN 1 85754 547 8

The publisher acknowledges financial assistance
from the Arts Council of England

Set in Monotype Garamond by XL Publishing Services, Tiverton
Printed and bound in England by SRP Ltd, Exeter

Acknowledgements

Acknowledgements are made to the editors of the following publications in which some of these poems have appeared:

A Commonplace Book (Carcanet Press), Acumen, Agenda, Connections, Dream Catcher, Exeter Poetry Prize Anthology 1998 (Odyssey Press), *Gargoyle, Last Words* (Picador), *Making Worlds* (Headland), *Moving Worlds, Mslyexia, Orbis, Other Poetry, PN Review, Poetry London, Poetry Review, The Art of Life* (Lawrence & Wishart), *The Independent on Sunday, The Tabla Book of New Verse 1999, Wasafiri.*

'Eden' was commissioned for National Poetry Day and broadcast on BBC Radio 4 and BBC Knowledge; 'The Fabergé Egg' was commissioned by the Salisbury Festival for display in jewellers. 'Don't ask me, love, for that first love' was commissioned for the BBC Poetry Proms and broadcast on Radio 3.

Several poems were written for The Royal Mail during a residency as part of the Poetry Society's Poetry Places scheme. I am grateful to both organisations.

Contents

I

II

III

I

The Chine

To be back on the island is to be
cast adrift but always facing the same
mother who stays ashore, is always there
despite the mist. My balcony's a crib.
Through its bars the waves rush in. Not a ship,
not a gull, and the sky in its slow revolve
winding the Isle of Wight with a giant key.

We are spinning backwards in a slow spin;
we are in a time warp, a gap, a yawn,
a chine that cleaves the mind in two, a line
on the land's belly. Shanklin. Rhylstone Gardens
where an old man rolls tobacco, as spare
with the strands as the years have been with him.
Luccombe with its own chine, barely a stream.

Every childhood has its chine, upper world
and lower. Time itself seems vertical
and its name too implies both bank and stream.
To be back on the island is to walk
in both worlds at the same time, looking down
on talus, horsehair fern notched through the Ice Age,
Stone Age, Bronze Age and still here at our heels;

looking up like an elf, ears cocked to silence,
from a zigzag of silver and silt. A chine
is a form of urgency to reach the sea.
As coastlines have eroded, chines, like orphans
stranded in a high place without their slope
of history, have had to take a short cut,
make deep cuts into the soft clay of cliffs.

Childhood has its railings too. And its catches
of glove on rust, twisted wire with a slight give.
Playthings. For in an upper world that turns
beachfronts into toytowns, patches of moss
into stands of minuscule trees, no railing
is not a harp, no rung a wind might play on
something other than its maker intended.

Every leaf must be touched and tasted, holly
tested for suppleness, mimosa dusted.
The mind has its work cut out by the senses
and analogies must be drawn, the unknown
be known a friend by citing its kith and kin.
Shanklin: I know you as you were, the timbers
of your pier, now gone, of your tree-stormed bridges.

But in the lower world we dream. We listen.
Not for water which is the sound of listening
or for schoolgirls passing above unseen.
Under lawns, hotels, we sit hours midstream,
crouched under a hundred blankets. If eyes
were ears, we'd hear the very mud-bed thicken,
rise in little mounds where the water's clean.

Every path brings us back to the beginning.
Shanklin Chine is closed for the winter, both ends
barred with notices. But the mind is not.
Or memory. And time is spinning backwards
with the mainland out of sight and the great plain
where herds roamed the floor of the English Channel
and were drowned by it flush again with valleys.

I look down on them, my own that were fed
by chines, from the long esplanade of light
on Keats Green and seem to remember walking
with my mother here, running my hand on railings.
The beautiful inn on the corner's a wreck
and there, at the bend, where the light's so bright
and people walking down the steep incline

pause at the top before walking down, black
against the blaze before their torsos sink,
something vanishes, there, where the path drops
and a young boy comes running down the hill.
Never, O God, to be afraid of love
is inscribed on a new bench where I sit,
facing the headland with its crown in mist.

The Rain Chapel

We are roofed under rain. Rain so great
we imagine it a cave, a chapel of timber
drumming us to sing. Our breath comes short
and cranky. We are children learning hymns.

Rain stands over us, patient, obdurate,
rain has faith. Of unimaginable beauty
is the voice rain has in mind. Our part,
though here we are as quiet as mice, mutely

lifting eyes to the rapping of rain. Rain's eyes
are steady. So many eyes has a cave.
We look down, not abashed by our performance
but by our lack of faith. We try to believe

in the voice rain has in mind, for a soundboard
needs melody, melody man while we –
but we are children and children are afraid.
O who will sing the solo? She will, no she will

and someone always does. But in our heads
we hear a voice not so easily betrayed.
Rain eases off and leans back. Sways, pedals,
glances back to the exit. Shines on slate.

For every cave has an exit and even birds
sing better after rain. And there we file
to the music, gratefully, as the last chords
rise to the rafters, tearing off our veils.

Writing Letters

After chapel on Sundays we wrote letters,
ruling pencil lines on airmails. Addresses
on front and back often bearing the same name,
same initial even, for in some countries
they don't bother to draw fine lines between
family members with an alphabet.

Those who remembered their first alphabet
covered the page in reams of squiggly letters
while those who didn't envied them. Between
them was the fine line of having addresses
that spelt home, home having the ring of countries
still warm on the tongue, still ringing with their name,

and having addresses gone cold as a name
no one could pronounce in an alphabet
with no *k-h*. Some of us left our countries
behind where we left our names. Wrote our letters
to figments of imagination: addresses
to darlings, dears, we tried to tell between,

guessing at norms, knowing the choice between
warmth and reserve would be made in the name
of loyalty. As we learnt our addresses
off by heart, the heart learnt an alphabet
of doors, squares, streets off streets, where children's letters
felt as foreign as ours from foreign countries.

Countries we revisited later; countries
we reclaimed, disowned again, caught between
two alphabets, the back and front of letters.
Street names change; change loyalties: a king's name
for a saint's. Even the heart's alphabet
needs realignment when the old addresses

sink under flyovers and new addresses
never make it into books where their countries
are taken as read. In an alphabet
of silence, dust, where the distance between
darling and dear is desert, where no name
is traced in the sand, no hand writes love letters,

none of my addresses can tell between
camp and home, neither of my countries name
this alphabet a cause for writing letters.

Nostalgia

It's a night for nostalgia he said.
I felt I was missing something, some
echo of nights we must have shared
in separate alleyways, far off home

rain drew him back to, or clouds,
or the particular light behind rain.
I was nostalgic for words, last words
of a poem I would read on the train.

There was a power cut today. I lit
three candles, ate lamb and read
by candlelight. The beauty of it
was too lonely so I went to bed.

It rained then. In the daylight dark.
I lay there till I heard a click
and voices. When the lights came back
it was like a conjuring trick –

there they were, the animated creatures
of my life I had thought inanimate
objects. And I was the one conjured
out of their dream of a dark planet.

The Alder Leaf

It is perfect. And of a green so bright
no other green has a say in it, fine-veined
and tiny-toothed, in short, a leaf a child might
choose to love, remember. And later, name.
Children love what is perfect, the best catkin,
blossom with each whisker in place. But sometimes
on a path they will halt and bend to a matted
object strangely furred, spun with gauze but numb
to prodding and hard as rock, neither insect
nor larva, stone nor egg and troubled both
by choosing and ignoring it or failing
to find something on a nature trail, loath
to ask but asking, *what is it?* learn nothing
of shit too late to name in retrospect.

Writing Home

As far back as I remember, 'home'
had an empty ring. Not hollow, but visual
like a place ringed on a map, monochrome
in a white disc. Around it were the usual
laurel hedges, the chine, the hockey pitch,
the bridge. On one side, the crab-apple tree
with its round seat, whose name puzzled me, which
wasn't surprising since everyone but me
seemed to understand such things, take for granted
apples can't be eaten, crabs can be planted.

Writing home meant writing in that ring, mostly
to Mummy. Mummy had a white fur coat
and framed in it her face looked tired and ghostly.
I am very well and happy, I wrote,
meaning it. Sensing somewhere in that frame
a face too far away, too lost, to worry.
And why would I? Worry should keep, like shame,
its head down in dreams. Sorry sorry sorry
I can't write anymore goodbye love Mimi
I wrote after only four lines to Mummy.

There's no irony in that. I was six.
Right from the start, home was an empty space
I sent words to. Mapped my world, tried to fix
meanings to it. Not for me, but to trace
highlights someone could follow: Brownies, Thinking
Day, films, a fathers' hockey match, a play
called Fairy Slippers, picnics, fire drills, swimming.
Even the death of a King. When my birthday?
I wrote at the same time, dropping the 'is',
too proud of my new question mark to notice.

My mother kept all my letters for ten years,
then gave them back to me. Perhaps they never
touched her, were intended only for my ears
for I never knew her then or asked whether
she made sense of them, if my references
to the small world of a girls' school in England
had any meaning. It was the fifties. Suez,
Mossadegh, white cardies, Clarks sandals. And,
under the crab-apple tree, taking root,
words in a mouth puckered from wild, sour fruit.

Holiday Homes

It's that particular yellow of stone
I recognise, though this is Edward Hopper
destabilising, I'm told, perspective: a lone

house on a hill, its face to sun, a runner
of gold on lawn spilling down the embankment
on to sprays of cedar, I think they're cedar,

with their backs to me; a perspective lent,
not only by the train from which this scene
is seen, though without any sense of movement

bar those lightning stabs of an acid lime-green
striking the branches, but also lent by
the painter's memory to mine – one keen

and empirical, the other, like many
people's traumatised by displacement, poor
and generic. These people claim how happy

their childhoods were, paint pictures even more
static than this. Ask them the year, they flounder,
don't ask them to fit the pieces, their jigsaw

is made of sky and sky was never ground
pieced into fields. I'll take this home for mine,
it's like any number of homes I found

placed in the wind. Cypress, cedar or pine –
it's all the same to me. Out of the painting,
I'm out of here for good, leaving a line

of families I borrowed, mothers, siblings,
a railroad track that like all railroad tracks
keeps promising without delivering.

I hate this house on a hill; ocean, outback,
dark side wall where the man, like a cockerel
up at dawn, wheeling his barrow, comes tacking

back to the front with compost, potato peel,
his useless, toothless grin. Where are they all?
No one's out on the lawn. It's early still.

That yellow frontage doesn't fool me, level
horizon hiding sea: I know it's there,
I can smell it, hear cutlery, the table

groaning with ham and jam, tremendous stir
of family. Taste toothpaste mixed with toast.
I have lived their lives, been their daughter, sister,

dog-walker, skivvy, peeled potatoes, lost
days and weeks out of my life playing ping-pong,
hula-hoop in holiday homes, a guest

for Christmas, Easter, friend who tagged along
not for the fun but for the hell of it.
Hell was other people's kindness: belonging

served on a plate like someone else's favourite
food destined to become my own with each
plump sultana bursting against my palate.

It did no harm. Imagination teaches
the mind the same; and love of humankind,
recognising ourselves in others, reaches

from house to house, hill to hill: but mind
is not a heaven, bright blue dome to spend
one's days under, lazing; or any kind
of friendly roof when cedars sough in wind.

Sadness

It is difficult to know what to do with so much happiness
                                                Naomi Shihab Nye

With sadness there is something to rub against —
these, your words, for unhappiness is speechless.
Sad air breathes, at whatever altitude,
recirculating air. Rub it against glass

and the shape it takes is nothing but the melt
of breath. Follow it with your eyes along
the patterns of the curtains and it will trap you
in a leit-motif you can't escape. You're wrong.

When the world falls in around you, there are
no wounds to tend, holes to fill, no prop
of stubborn plaster; tenements don't crumble.
I've measured the ceiling for the curtain's drop,

metres are where I left them. *When the world
falls in around you, you have pieces to pick up,
something to hold in your hands* you say. Like this?
this button? A grey that fell, just now, a trick

of heaven? No, it comes from my green pyjamas.
Happiness sews on buttons. Sadness looks for
sadness to couple with, not comfort. The minute
I lift my head from the page, my heart takes over.

All Things Bright and Beautiful

No sooner do I wish for the random than
some pigeon comes belting out of the sky
towards me, is joined by another who squats
on the parapet while the first flies off,
gulls wheel above and a third pigeon comes
sidling round a drainpipe to make a pair.

Thoughts they might be in a mind like a sky
sometimes empty, sometimes – for here comes a flock
filling the window – active, frantic, cluttered.
More is due to luck than we like to think,
fearing the random, out of control, the mess
life without consequence would leave us with.

Remembering how in chapel the idea
of goodness, justice, was as palpable
as the doe, hare, small creatures hung above us
in a Tarrant watercolour, how hymns
and their mystifying words nonetheless rang
true as I would be in the vows I made,

as the faith that they and their keeping would
be welcome in the world – remembering,
in short, innocence, I find it so hard
to let go of the verb 'to beget' – how good
begets the greater good – to believe in luck,
good or bad, and against it, helplessness.

Where are the birds now? Drifting in a loop
like cinders. Roofed, I am under their wings,
overhead beating, gliding, or above them –
my dark fat pigeon on the guttering,
poking that black head out of his collar like
an idea not sure if it can make the distance.

Childhood Books

They always saw me through; kept me indoors
lying belly down on a counterpane,
stretching the hours on a single bed, poring

over cowboy annuals frame by frame,
The Famous Five, Black Beauty, Little Women –
scores of books remembered only by name

and the room, atmosphere I read them in.
It was a shared room and the maroon carpet
where I spilt black ink, the guilt of it, summon

a room-mate calling, *aren't you coming out yet,*
when are you coming out? and with it, all
the turmoil and agony books create

while a ball thuds against an outside wall,
the sound of sevensies echoes on stone,
I fall behind in coordination skills

but run ahead past endings to the questions
endings leave you with, answers you supply,
authoring every journey but your own.

For what was mine but a hole in the sky,
a non-event, half a wing in a window?
Did sun glint on its rivets? Did I fly

by myself, was there land or sea below?
Or simply a drop to the answers I wrote
too young to have answers, too long ago?

Today I'm infinitely sad. Afloat
with nothing to attach my sadness to.
Though it's March and nearly too mild for coats.

And ground is sad, sad for us who are no
gazelles – how long it takes to cover paving
stones. How rarely we run and then only to

catch or miss a train, I never liked running
not even then – long before I smoked.
You can't run and be sad I suppose. Being

sad's like finishing a brilliant book.
Becoming aware of the time, the room.
That tear-stained patch on the pillow. Stroking

the pillowcase, between finger and thumb
tweezering a quill that had scratched your cheek,
pulling it out to unruffle the plume.

Sometimes a tuft of balding down was stuck
to the shaft. Sometimes a blade, speckled, dipped
and blew, too limp to use. It all comes back.

How you tickle a feather along your lips,
lick them, balance moustaches under your nose;
stick with a snap barbs that cross over, slip

into troughs like a zip whose teeth won't close;
then with all the flight gone out of its vanes
how you drop it, knowing no one will know.

How a whole life, a whole childhood can drain
away without someone to see it go.
And yet, here's a hole I remember plain
as the day: a pinprick left in the pillow.

Lyric

A lyric couldn't do what birds do, could it,
alighting at random, swinging from line
to line, driving at the reader. Some birds
against buildings, grey on grey, disappear
entirely, dying in and out of colour,
or white-winged, black-winged, differentiate
too briefly to inhabit the memory
of such a small three-dimensional plane.

Birds seem designed to be seen against sky.
As the lyric is designed to be seen
against self. Slanted on a background where
whatever matches blends and is interred,
whatever holds its own ground, black or white,
argues depth and whatever hovers, craves
descent, struggling to alight on a skyline
but failing, having to fly, flies out of frame.

Simorgh

for Carcanet's thirtieth anniversary

Simorgh sat on top of the Tree of All Seeds,
beating her wings, causing the seeds to fall
at the feet of thirty birds. Of *si morgh*,
as we would say. But whatever the language,
however far-flung, birds follow the fling
of seed and so did they. Round the globe, singly
but in tandem, she led them to the world's end.
Who are you? they cried, from raven to wren,
and what are we that have journeyed in fog
and suffered these wounds on the way? And *Simorgh*
replied, rubbing her feathers on each wound,
not as we would salt but as healing rain would
plumes of glass: See, your wounds are wiped and with them
the space between *si morgh* that hides my name.

Listening to Strawberry

for Aubrey ('Strawberry') de Selincourt

I knew it as the poetry I could never hear
without his voice to give it utterance
and the way it ran inside me was clearer,
closer, than the way it ran in others

though they loved it too, owned it too
but owning so much else, loved it that much less.
Owning so little now, I recall how he drew
it out with pipesmoke, through long crossed legs

out of the earth as if he, so long and lean,
were a brook for the vowels to run through,
knocking consonants like little stones
to quaver in their wake. Certainty can quaver too.

And still retain its faith. Outcast
in its deepest spells of orphanhood, the soul
can recall – through memories of grass
and place, a shaking hand on a pipe's bowl

that indicates a turn of phrase – an undertow
to weather, a companionship that being human,
echoing high in leafy woods, confiding low
when at our lowest, deprived of human company,

makes deprivation sweet to bear. And for
those of us who heard him, in our girlhoods
when girlhood was still a word to stand for
a kind of kingdom, a wreath around our heads,

it was a binding that netted us together
like wild strawberries never safe from bird
or hand; a murmur I can still remember
with or without remembering the words.

Middle Age

There are those who are radiant confronting
death in cornflower blues and violets.
There are roofs that kneel to large shapes of sun
submissively as cows to the sky's gait.
I protect myself from happiness, rooting
into the search for it, mourning its youth,
though it's the lesser courage that admits
to unhappiness, to gladness, the greater.
What did we vow we'd be in middle age? –
young of course. Immortal. Assuming process
reversible by that effort of will
only gods possess, protean, promethean.
Knowing we'd die but not knowing how tired
we'd get, even of loving, how we'd fear
emotion. No one tells us. How we'd get
our second wind from death and even then
only those who are charmed, transformed by grace
we think a miracle – who knows what strength
it takes, who only sees those blue eyes bluer,
who only sees apparel. No one tells us
about middle age. Forget teeth, sight, hearing,
what about the heart? You'd think it a dumb
organ, stones in its well, a clobbered clock
not knowing moments from minutes, stone itself.
I tell my heart to move, it doesn't. Look,
I say, what do you like out there, tail feathers?
It looks but doesn't see, sees but can't name.
It's middle-aged. I think of Keats and wonder
how one so young could feel it rich to die
till I remember illness, pain. And though
here I am healthy, knowing pain will pass,
from where I am I catch the drift of it –
a wind that blows the other way. Or rather,
doesn't blow but being ever more easeful,
makes me see, as if in a glassy surface,
fingers dragged in the shallows of its wake.

River Sonnet

Welling up in her fingers, water runnelled
seaward through stones. She wasn't watching water.
Or thinking of tomorrow – how time funnelled,
flows. Water was doing her thinking for her.
Draining down her thoughts till they ran as lightly
as leaves across a playground, rose to torment
branches that had borne them, betrayed them, nightly
blurred distinctions, daily held to their bent
and finally torn loose. She heard the river
babble, level, contradictions resolve in
a rush, out of her hands, felt quarrels fly
in droves. *Who-o-o* the river sang, *who-so-ever*
clouds rang round the sky, sky thinking itself in
river, river thinking itself in sky.

Gooseberries

Birds are chirping now rain has stopped, their songs
like the rain are silver. I hear the silence,
the music of panic, of loneliness.
Rain passes like unhappiness and birds
sing happily out of the same dull silver.
It is all the silvers of cloud and cold,
the white shine of illness. A friend lies dying
in hospital. The night I saw her there
we watched fireworks from her window, her window
filled with photos and dried flowers for real
flowers are infectious, fireworks at Christmas.
When two times meet, another friend says, stories
must end – by which he means, when day meets dusk,
the page must be marked, the book closed and children
while away their questions. I heard a story
of a child who, it was foretold, would die
when the leaves began to fall; when they did,
a sister, brother, sewed the leaves back on
but how the story ended wasn't told –
besides, the dying do not want our questions.
Today I bought a card with berries, currants,
each translucent as a small wineglass held
against light, each tiny globe marbled, jewelled.
The flurry of birdsong behind the curtain
has gone: now and then the trill of a latecomer.
Every morning I wake alone. Today
I find the balm and bitterness. The sweetness
of pulp, pop of a taut skin, gooseberries
a friend on the phone tells me a hen used to
lay eggs under, two eggs you'd have to slide
on your belly to reach so prickly was
the bush, with hairs sun shone through on the berries
fine as the hairs on the back of a child's hand.
Twice a day two times meet. Between the two,
like a prayer between two palms, the bookmark,
the memory, is placed. When day meets night,
night meets day, we must hold our breath, delay
our need for answers, live with what comes next.

II

The Inwardness of Elephants[1]

for Aamer Hussein

The Wishing Tree

Where do those poems go, the ones
we wake from, take back to sleep and oblivion?
In what book have they been written?

How deep and dark the book, how full,
how cavernous – a book of all the ages,
grey fish crossing the open page.

It's Christmas Day. I've been given
a wishing tree. Wishes hang from its branches
like silver fish, wishing me stardust and linen

robes, golden moons and skylarks, bright
coloured sandals and tinkling sounds like Ariel's:
it's a poem, a red heart beating in a well.

Three elephants walk the rim and chocolate coins
I will never eat ring the earthenware. I'm caught
between the two – between air and water,

heaven and hell. I sing better
in the air. Underwater I am dream and agony,
sin and righteousness – who am I

in the ocean's depth? *And may your God hold you
in the palm of his hand*, one of my wishes
ends with. It went right through me. Something Irish.

Who is this God who holds my fields in rain?
I think of his palm. Of Iran. The gold
hand of Fatima I gave a friend on a chain.

My wishing tree's gone dark. Gone the way
those poems go. Underwater it bursts into flame.
On it is hung my God, my friends, their names.

I've been reading Vendler on Graham
mornings in bed. They're blending together,
weaving in and out of each other

like seaweed through surf.
I don't know which road to take
into my daughter's flesh. And if,

inadvertently, I come upon a snapshot
stuck on a fridge of two small boys in shorts
– one small, one heartbreakingly big

for I remember slipping hands under his armpits,
hoisting him up and how T-shirts twist
and everyone thinks he's older than he is

in those great big feet – then my whole
week gets skewed and I'm guaranteed
bad dreams. Unravelling skeins, skies, bleeding

into water, over my head, under my hips.
This is how I lose a daughter,
how I make red water wield the whip.

These are the body's tokens,
this is how the spirit is broken
night after night, dream after dream.

I've bought myself a watercolour. A sunset
and silhouettes. A mother and her calf, two trees
and a flat horizon. Strange humps like refugees

huddle on their backs. They can't be towers.
What are those humps? I asked her brother.
They have passed one tree, they will pass the other.

Mammont

Long before the mammoth there was
mammont, an enormous creature
with feet resembling a bear's.

In Estonian, *maa* and *mutt*
mean 'earth' and 'mole' and indeed
mammont lived underground, ate mud

and sometimes on subterranean walks
poked its head above ground
only to duck back down for it found

sunlight hurtful, so hurtful
it perished in the open air.
Elephants still hate the glare.

But in moonlight
they spray themselves with water
and discreetly, under its fountain, mate.

Are you the year's last sun then,
husband? snow in your hair?
It's a long time since we've spoken.

Once, long ago, at the mouth
of the Lena river, a mammoth
was found with an eye and brain

still intact after isatis, wolverines,
foxes had fed on it and skinned,
the remains were sent to St. Petersburg

where they fuelled endless debate.
The body, however mutilated,
records what the mind forgets.

Films about the British Empire
are invariably monochrome – sepia – the colour
of tea and biscuits my son says and we laugh

in one of my fields of tenderness.
He himself is a field. Taller than
the tallest grasses, higher than the highest

mast in a bay. He faces the horizon,
hides his eyes by facing the other way.
He has tried travel. The song of whales.

He himself is the music he cannot play.
I am the wrong note he says. I change
my tune but I'm no piper, and my range

smaller than my strength belies and my breath
smokier every day. Of all the songs earth's
creatures sing, I aspire to the elephant's rumble

too bass for man to hear. Because it covers
distance, because it moves the herd. Mothers
are always wrong. Whatever the song,

whatever the note of anger, love, despair.
And their song travels deep inside them,
down to their boots, down to the roots they tear.

My son stares out of his eyes as if to torch
his brain. He covers his head in a towel
for the world is covered with jawbones, burial

grounds the thaw reveals, I look like
Elephant Man he says. He eats his meal.
Potatoes mostly. Shovels them through the crack.

Back from India, my daughter gives me
a carved filigree elephant, a baby
inside it tooled from the same grey flesh.

Is it ivory? I ask, as if chinoiseries,
chessmen, dominoes, combs, piano keys,
daggers, rifle butts, hunting horns,

inlaid pulpits and mosque doors, Zeus
at Olympia, Athena in the Parthenon,
Tutankhamun's chair, Solomon's throne,

weren't enough white gold plundered,
not to mention hair and tails turned
into fly whisks, ears into tables,

feet into umbrella stands and even
eyelashes sold to guarantee fertility
and the desired number of children.

No, she says. And my cow proliferates.
On boxes, bedspreads, mugs, cushions,
in jasper, wood, brass, ceramic processions.

My favourite elephants are on a black
glasses case: two calves embroidered
in shades of pink, one rose on powder,

the other reversed. I attract them the way
I do children: a whole orphanage of elephants
on presents, cards, surrounds me on my birthday

and from Oregon come cuttings – Chendra
has anaemia, Pet eye surgery, and in Kenya,
when there is no ivory, there are no orphans.

Buddha

Queen Sirimahamaya
was the most beautiful of women.
No pedestal was ever placed higher,

no purity deemed whiter
than hers. One summer night by the light
of the full moon, she dreamed

she was transported to a palace
on the peak of the Himalayas.
There, she had a dream in which

a silvery-white elephant descended
from the mountains, entered
her room and bowed down before her.

In its trunk it bore a lotus.
Impregnated, the Queen gave birth
to the fruit of the divine phallus

under a tree in the tranquillity
of the Lumbini Garden.
Such was Buddha's reincarnation.

I tell you this for no reason other than
that it's delightful. I've stolen it.
I envy her. The zipless fuck. The man

and not the God, the sex and not
the birth. Speechlessness. Though
in real life it was precisely that

I objected to, oh where were the words?
How many deaths I died in silence.
In God it is meet, in man, violence.

is one of the saddest roads remember?
that leads to everything, so Breton said:
el camino where a traveller,

slumped in his saddle, wanders;
a motorway in Sophia where a cyclist's scarf
flutters; by a stream you hear laughing

and catching a glimpse of, wonder
how a stream so small and dry
could dream itself a river:

all the roads you have ever sung to,
fought back tears in, helped a blind man
cross and crossed again,

all our sad processions, down to the very
smallest, on some dry
and dusty shelf.

Mothers dip their nose to a baby's scalp
like animals at water. Come up for air.
I smelt a sweetness in your hair,

close to the scalp, something like
stale cake. I smelt blossom on the landing
and thought of Louise Glück

– mock orange – asking how could she
rest with that odour in the world?
I fed the lemon tree you gave me

summer food for citrus then the clocks changed.
Through the barking of the dog
I sensed the length of its chain.

Darling

Darling was a word I used to throw
casually downstairs. Catch! a ball
big as a child's head bouncing lower

step by step. Down in the dank
of the cellar, under the jut of planks
and legs, lies something warm and friendly,

approachable as fur.
Whose is the voice of poetry,
the animal's or the keeper's?

There I am, small, dark, wordless
but something bright and shining
in me wanting to be heard.

The world is full of infrasound –
sudden flight, a meal abandoned.
Crossing a ford at sundown, the herd,

each mother with her calf shielded
from the arrow, a hide
too thick for arrows, a field

of tenderness, pit of spears.
What will you make of it, keeper?
Catch these tears.

This is where I am
in the smoke of a cigarette.
Darling, sweetheart, angel, poppet,

I wreathed them in, children, husbands.
Protect me! I demanded
and they disappeared.

The Wedding

I dream I am to be married.
A big affair. I search the grounds
for the groom – there are flowers, garlands,

stepped lawns, strangers everywhere.
Down some steps, a room dark as a mausoleum.
The doors are open. They sit prepared.

The family dead. Undead.
My favourite aunt who has broken off
relations, great-aunts, grandmother, stiff

as statues, old as Methuselah.
And where were you at the wedding?
Groom, husband, the only male.

Entombed in your own nightmares:
a mammoth once on the family
roof and you saving us; once, an animal

you said was the most beautiful thing
you had ever seen, rising
from a lake. And someone knifed it,

knifed it in the eye, a boy
you saw running in the distance, but all
I saw was moonlight, lake, animal,

a unicorn rising like a lady,
a knife, a flash, someone running and you
were that someone, yours was the beauty

you couldn't bear. We are who we dream of,
we are who we dream of, I tell myself over
and over when I am plagued by nightmares.

We trust each our own elephant
till our own elephant kills us.
The attendants holding the silk umbrellas,

the one who plies the fan
of peacock feathers, the man
with the flyswatter of yaktails.

You cannot cheat on the amount of oil
poured in the lamps for an elephant
will always honour the pace of the ritual.

Nor is the elephant's love less manifest.
He will insert his trunk, like a hand,
inside your garments and caress your breast.

He will follow, with his mate,
the undulations in B minor of *Iphigenia in Tauris*
or, on solo bassoon, *Oh, my Tender Musette.*

And the cow will stroke him with her long
and flexible member before bringing
it back upon herself, pressing its finger

first in her mouth, then in his ear.
While over their transports, whistling fire,
the harmony of two human voices

falls like summer rain.
Meat that walks like a mountain
among giant flowers, huge nettles and lobelia.

Child, don't be afraid.
The circle of nine precious stones
is never absent from his forehead.

1 I have drawn and collaged material for this sequence from *The Life and
Lore of the Elephant* by Robert Delort (Thames & Hudson, 1992).

Villanelle

No one is there for you. Don't call, don't cry.
No one is in. No flurry in the air.
Outside your room are floors and doors and sky.

Clocks speeded, slowed, not for you to question why,
tick on. Trust them. Be good, behave. Don't stare.
No one is there for you. Don't call, don't cry.

Cries have their echoes, echoes only fly
back to their pillows, flocking back from where
outside your room are floors and doors and sky.

Imagine daylight. Daylight doesn't lie.
Fool with your shadows. Tell you nothing's there,
no one is there for you. Don't call, don't cry.

But daylight doesn't last. Today's came by
to teach you the dimensions of despair.
Outside your room are floors and doors and sky.

Learn, when in turn they turn to you, to sigh
and say: You're right, I know, life isn't fair.
No one is there for you. Don't call, don't cry.
Outside your room are floors and doors and sky.

The Piano

You have found your digital metronome.
Where, you didn't say. I have never said,
or always said in so many words, how a piano
is nothing to the weight I bear. Your throat
so soft, feet bare, where you played the violin
in pyjamas, and the black and white cat whose instinct
for camouflage would draw him to the stool
when we weren't there – you didn't find it there.

Downstairs. On the ground floor of our lives.
Nor, in a flat whose floors walk into trees,
was it anywhere near the old metronome,
broken, mechanical, you'd repositioned;
flung aside with your oval clock I rescued,
reassembled, dismissed the missing sliver
of glass no one'll notice. The piano tuner
didn't steal it then. – Just as well.

A body is a thing of dread. A thing
of guilt. Desire and dream. Something
to purge with percussion. How rare it is
to merge with, to have your own organs sing
through another's. See, it has taken blindness
from your touch, the grime you took from newsprint,
down escalator rails. Milk will revive
its ivory. It must be cared for in silence.

And even a piano must have water.
Be tempered to the precise pitch of health.
How it hurts you. Hurts where you have already
hurt yourself. It is in step. I will take
the shawl it has worn so long only washing,
ruining will remove its folds and dents.
I don't want to remove them. Such a worn-in
fit is rare. I am cold. I'm cold, Tom, play.

Winter Dawn

Winter dawn has more doom than dawn in it.
Words on your lips. Dream words that made you wake.
That you must now translate. And born in it,
in winter dawn, out of a language like
the one you can't remember, like a lamb
being licked into shape, a child-self, the child
you spoke those dream words to, will say 'I am
what you said I am, though I'm not the child
you thought to comfort in your dream, small boy,
your boy, but you, you as a child, as lost,
and just as brave.' But it's hard to enjoy
your own voice sounding like a therapist
and not at all like telling a child you love,
a child who's wracked, *I think you're very brave.*

Terrapin

My daughter's fish are fine, she says,
three so small they haven't yet
changed colour; two fantails.

In shortening light our days
will be nosed through glass,
an afterglow of holiday.

She's got two tanks now.
One for fish, one
for a terrapin she's rescued.

They take up all her
living room, what with
friends crashing out, a father

for a lodger. They're thinking
of buying a boat, *don't*
I'm dying to say. Boats sink.

One I heard of left no trace
but a teddy bear floating on the canal –
true or not, boatpeople are always

saving cats, scraping hulls
and sooner or later moving into flats
they take months to redecorate.

Time my son moved out. Where to?
Where'll he put his piano? Who'd
put up with it? Round and round we go

swapping rooms, beds. September's
my own aquarium I was going to say.
My memory's getting short as a fantail's.

Writing on the back of a hand
as if ink in the blood could silt
the flow, flow swamp detail.

The Event

'Draw a floor plan of your childhood house,
place a cross in one room, write the event.'

If the cross were a single star – for stars
these nights come singly – on a paper flower
I could fish out of black waters, if water
didn't wash out ink, ink was magic ink
forgotten languages were written in
and memory the floor where I could kneel,
unfold and smooth the crumpled sheet, decipher
over a flame the starword, codeword, godword,
I would. Believe you me I would. I'd pore
with all the strength my eyes, wits, left half, right half
of my brain could muster over that crease,
cross, whatever the sign, could be a sound,
bell, cry, to lead me backwards to a street,
house, this one not that one, this with the trellis,
through its door with that same brass knocker, up
those worn blue treads. Floor plans would be no problem.
Never mind the event. I know what that is,
it's the poem. This one and every other,
happening, sprouting, coming up like nettles
in a rash of words. I've lost heart in them.
Today is my daughter's birthday. My pregnant
daughter, sleeping daughter. I'll let her sleep
her sickness off. I feel sleepy myself.
(When she wakes, your baby wakes, lift her
up to the windowsill, to her red giraffe
and watch her widen eyes of pure grey slate.)

Babies

There ought to be another word for babies.
Painters should paint them like women, the size
of continents, cloud formations, whales, Bacon
should have been their high priestess, specialised
in mounds of pink, primal soup of pink, muscled,
boned, straining away from buckles and braces;
dropped on all fours, teetering at odd angles
to exit from canvas, howling in cages.
There ought to be a God, capable of
metamorphosing into every hurdle
of a dream: a heel on the rung above
your hand, a Lucifer under your heel.
There ought to be a word, a God, for us:
us mothers, protectors, dreamers, creators.

Il Bacio Deli

for Sara

A baby, brown as its mother is blonde,
sits gurgling at the table next to me
under the yellow awning of the new
lilac café. It must be statutory.
The last time I was here a mother sat
with her newborn, her husband, a pregnant friend
and hers. Soon, Sara, you will be among them.
Young mothers smiling in the shade of cafés.

I liked the day we sat in the pub garden
– under an apple tree I think it was –
with a wasp Brian said liked Branston pickle.
The way you asked sharp questions at the printer's.
And how you smile, dimpled. Whenever I sit
in a café or park I've always said
– and did perhaps that day at High Wycombe –
babies swarm round me like wasps, noisy, sticky,

with their noisier but not so sticky mothers.
I came here to write, in peace and quiet; despite
the traffic, to rest my eyes tired from reading
poems to e-mail at the Royal Mail
and hundreds more for competitions. A bus
draws up, almost at my feet but I still hear
that mother and her baby going bye bye
bye bye, call and response, jingling a rattle.

They're staying though, while she bounces a foot,
clean as only a child's can be who has yet
to flip-flop pavements, know what bye bye means
and not to smile at strangers. Sara, I wish you
many cafés, and may strangers smile on you
and your child, as they will, and you smile back
as you will, knowing a grandmother's smile
when you see one, knowing we're never strangers.

The Suzuki Method

When I was nine they gave me
a half-sized violin and half-sized feelings.
When you were seven we gave you
a Cornflakes packet sellotaped
to a ruler. We gave you footsteps,
placed them in a boat and asked you
to stand in them. You stood.

You rowed your boat lightly,
jerkily, according to the numbers.
All the mothers in the class
were charged with the same numbers.
You stood in a fleet
of boats. You learned
to find your balance.

The fleet sailed.
Some boats capsized.
Some are sailing still in all weathers.
In the meantime, the mothers
forgot the numbers. Sometimes
at the bottom of an escalator
they heard them played by buskers.

Your feet are calloused now
with white callouses. Perhaps
they're fungal. And your
lips are white with foam.
No one wipes them.
They have given you medication
to give you half-sized feelings

– Yehuda Amichai's words.
I cut the pills in half
but even half a pill's enough
to fell an elephant.
I listen for your breath.
Cot death. Now you are twenty-six.
And I am fifty-seven.

Eden

In this country, nature is green on green.
In mine, green grows out of ochre, fawn, dun –
what are the colours of dust? Caught between
fruit trees what are they but shifts of the sun?

In this country, grass and tree are implicit
in each other, as in water. In mine,
dust and tree are awkward friends who elicit
only the same blessings at the same shrine.

But it's dust that deepens shadows, the tree
that plays on colours watermarked by shade.
When shade is deep as water, roots drink deeply,
and drinking from the same pool, friends are made.

If only we were dust and tree. My children,
grown from my poor soil. I imagined Eden.

III

Life in Art

With the simplicity of frost,
the muddy depths of dream
you can't recall and yet, lost
as they are, they gleam

with the clarity of snowflakes
melting under a eye,
an ambiguity that wakes
to rain's late lullaby

with words as small as pronouns you
or I could take as ours,
a big heart and an old one, new
only in its scars

the way a thistle's colour draws
a thumb along its brush
and tells you it's not spiny wars
but softness that can crush

the way children know breath rises
like white manes in the mist
and lovers look for no surprises
on lips so often kissed

with these and other ways in mind
I might seduce a verse
to wake to, speak with, touch and find
that poetry's no worse

for frost and mud, snow and rain,
the languages of war,
of love that fears to hear again
abuse it's heard before.

I might renew acquaintance, mend
walls I never breached
or breach them now and not pretend
I practised what I preached.

I might forget my small concerns,
leaning against the jamb,
watching the world go by that turns
me into what I am.

And as for larger griefs – well, they
are the dumb stones in my heart.
They will not speak nor I betray
life in art.

Snails

Thousands there must have been, scaling the wall,
hanging from stems like sloths, lined under thistles.
Two were coupled. One slid along the coping
inch by endless inch, many waved their horns
as if in dream and in the undergrowth were
hosts of them, households hidden from inspection.
I stood staring, horrified, fascinated,
horror dissolving into something close
to tenderness. I walked to the Post Office
on the watch for them. Other gardens, driveways,
clumps of weed by railings, everything, even
the people, seemed peculiarly bare. As if
there were too few of us, too much space,
as if Stoke Newington were a new country
and I should be glad to be living here.

The Fabergé Egg

Lilies of the Valley Easter Egg, 1898

It is born as a shape, the shape of birth.
    Always the same shape but no sooner born
than form, the buried form spring must unearth,
    must make new, however timeless or timeworn,
calls to its maker: 'What am I, what am I
    beyond my shell? Am I fish or fowl, flower
        or fruit, whose roots are these, whose clay? What lies
            in my white mortuary,
        rocking, crowning through slippages that shower
        stones on my head?' And its maker replies:

'These are the hands I have trained for you, these
    their veins. Running across the grain, so thin
not one runs straight. Let them run with the ease
    of grasses, tendrils, stems, over the skin
I stretch for you, look, against the light, fine
    as pink enamel, how the sun's glow steals
        through each soft web, soft as a fontanelle.
            See how my fingers shine?'
    Form nods its head. And each nod breaks, peals
        into a lily of the valley bell.

Bells so true to life, life's put in the shade.
    'In these fonts I'll christen you in ablutions
of gold rivers, turn you through ruby, jade,
    diamond, pearl, rockcrystal revolutions.
And under the crown that will spread your fame
    with three Easter kisses, a "Christ is risen,"
        "Yes Christ is truly risen," I'll install
            heads in a threefold frame.
    Who but a goldsmith would think to imprison
        their likenesses in such a small cathedral!

The Czarina, she'll thank me for it. Olga,
   Tatiana, their father Nicholas . . .
As for these hands that work as well in vulgar
   gunmetal, on copper pots, nickel, brass
shell casings and grenades – it's not your hoard
   or your precious stones a new world will praise
      when a mother's love has bitten the dust
                  and you're banished abroad
but these, their skill.' There's no response. Buds raise
   their heads and hang them. Droop as lilies must.

The Love Barn

Remember the swallows – or were they
swifts? – in the love barn where the wooden
rail we peered over might have been
the height waves tip out of over
rocky pools or the bar of a certain
Sicilian café scattering waiters
like birds or the fence of a driveway
where lupins grow tall as you were
in the barnlight where we stood, leaning
over a railing, smelling the hay.

The Coat

I'm travelling to meet you, through a long
black tunnel with one strip of yellow light
into the New Year. A good year, this one,
I feel it in my bones. Warm in red fleece
and my fingers red with bad circulation.

How we've circled each other through the years,
travelling north to south and back again.
Waited for light at the end of the tunnel.
It flashes on my paper. Sunstrobe. Flickers,
steadies, flickers again. I lift my eyes

to red housing estates, soft greys and greens
of England. How lovely it is to travel
on a quiet Saturday. And tomorrow
I'll be on the train again, heading home,
missing you and most likely knocked off-centre.

We must have reached an impasse. Lovely to
stop, draw breath, lift eyes to the russet golds
of embankments, purples of winter branches
and only on ploughed fields the dearth of colour
I take for granted travelling on trains.

How small the houses are. How sweet it is
vanishing out of a weekend. I see
too many colours to name. How quietly
they talk me down, gainsay my view of England.
Do the same. Quietly so I don't notice.

Wear me down, my view of you. As you meet me
at the other end. In your new warm coat
that doesn't fit. What colour? Not brown again.
Not black, not grey, I'll leave a space I'll fill in
later. Here _____. (We've just arrived at Luton.)

Just to Say

I miss you – let me count the ways –
morning, noon and night;
I miss you on my darkest days
and when things for once go right.

I miss you in the inbetweens,
in shades of grey and gaps,
like bowling-alleys miss their greens,
lost mariners their maps.

I miss you like the tide its mark,
a church its congregation,
Londoners a place to park,
refugees their nation.

My old mistrust gives up the ghost,
my new misfortunes don't,
I miss the boat, the bank, the last post,
the film, the joke, the point.

I'm a misfit in my own skin,
a fist without a glove,
a bow without a violin,
an amoeba in love.

Counting pebbles on the shore,
I'm splitting hairs much finer
to mount up ways I miss you more
than all the tea in China.

I'm Christmas without mistletoe,
a firework missing fire,
so lost without my Romeo
I'd settle for the friar.

Yes, a misbegotten mismatch,
a score without a song
for a good-time girl in a bad patch,
a ding without a dong.

I missed my chance, I threw away
the line and missed my cue
the day you rang me just to say
miss you, miss you, miss you . . .

Moving the Bureau

for The Philatelic Bureau, Edinburgh

I've never owned a bureau. If I had,
I'm sure I'd move it. I move everything.
Compulsively. I'm not sure I even know
what a bureau is. But what furniture
I do have, moves and I move with it. Dance
with it really, left, right, left right left, up
to the skirting board, back into the chimney.

And then admire it. See who else to dance with.
I'm sure a bureau would be admirable
in its tact and adaptability.
All those cubbyholes. And drawers and flaps.
I could keep my stamps in it. First day covers,
Millennium issues, letters, cards, catalogues,
bulletins, bills, then move the whole shebang

again if necessary. Which it would be.
Size is never what it seems at first glance.
The first dance never wholly innocent.
And once you've moved one thing, everything
shifts: that play of light on the wall, the way
your hips swerve corners, even in the dark,
and your hand unerringly finds the switch.

Even the way you think or don't think changes.
But once you've done the tango, quickstep, mastered
the paso doble with a fridge, a bureau's
nothing. A Nureyev. Baryshnikov.
Lord of the Sword Dance, of the Highland Fling.
Hermes on heels with impossible wings.
A bureau's a beau with a secret spring.

Song

I have landed
as if on the wing
of a small plane.

It is a song I have
landed on that barely
feels my weight.

Sky is thick with wishes.
Regrets fall down
like rain.

Visit me.
I am always in
even when the place

looks empty,
even though the locks
are changed.

Tenderness

I washed the grapes, let clear water run through them
till my nails went numb, gave them hours to drip
lopsidedly from sieve to sink while I rinsed
the small Greek cucumbers, laid them in rows,
patted them dry, sluiced the fat vine tomatoes.

I did this for you. Took you in my mouth.
Lingered over you. Ridges rose along
your feet, ribbed them like miniature canoes.
I lay still on the shore. Not talking, smiled
as you rabbited on, your gripes, your jokes.

I aged myself as slowly as I dared,
once in a while suggested walks. Waylaid you
under the young acacia, looking up
into a word for green that was a word
for gold. Let you sleep to a silent phone.

Now you house me. Stumble on my misnomers
under the kick of language, catch my drift
in a chance remark and hurry me home.
Tenderness, ah tenderness, you observe,
on the tip of your tongue, a hint of cachou.

I am the silk page at your fingertips
running down on me, the fruit you revolve
and leave mapped in bloom, the blur of a lens
you lift a shirt hem to, rub over, breathe on,
I am the way you see the world anew.

Love in an English August

Twice I've gone as far as the High Street phone.
For no good reason. But to rein in passion.
August in London. Making time my own.
For while sun comes and goes, love is on ration,

lying open to the weather, on heat,
on hold. And I was never one for half-
way houses, never did learn to compete
with mild-mannered sisters, cope with rebuff,

temper quarrels with jokes. Freak storms with sighs
like small rain when drought's at the door. False comfort
to borrow heat from the sun when sun lies
under leaf, heat under cold. 'Temperate'

let's call it, for it cuts both ways, this trope
to prove even a full sun brings false hope.

To prove even a full sun brings false hope,
largesse earns little thanks, recall a cot
we broke, you mended, badly, as if rope
could hold together sleep as delicate

as that, a corner cupboard, big red cushions,
yellow mugs, the colour and history
two people meeting late in life might fashion
a new life with, leftovers of a party

the other wasn't party to till later
in the kitchen, when salad's at its best,
telling it how it really was, they savour
rich pickings, scrape the trifle bowl and test

the water, breakages, take out the trash.
For no good reason. But to rein in passion.

For no good reason, but to rein in passion
or rather, give it free rein, for without it
how can I swing goodbyes, stroll from the station
late at night under trees and sing about it,

how can I not 'concentrate on you'?
Perhaps, like that letter I wrote from school
about a fancy dress party, it's true:
to win a prize all you need do is truly

'consantrait'. I never knew – I've just looked it
up – I was going as a wedding cake.
And you, marking your one Lottery ticket
do, I recall, pause, concentrate. Good luck.

And keep it. My share I mean. Strictly on loan.
August in London. Making time my own.

August in London. Making time my own.
So quick to tell me everybody steals it
and I let them, where are you thief? Don't groan.
Own up. Where's my life, what thicket conceals it,

where've you put a decade and more, my prime,
my time with the children out of my hair,
over the hill and far away, that chime
of my maligned spinsterhood? Is it there,

under those papers, books you never read
or, tired of good intentions, pitched like tents,
dropped out of diaries, left lying in bed
with clothes? Come clean thief, where? And where's the sense

in playing for time? Here, sign the confession.
For while sun comes and goes, love is on ration.

For while sun comes and goes, love is on ration?
Can paupers then imagine, when sun's nailed
to the spot, rimmed round with fire, that creation
might decree free rations at least till sun's sailed

out of sight? No chance. So don't hold a glass
up to sky. Love's chained to a rock, come rain,
come shine, and heartache's been put out to grass.
But if sun's nailed to the spot and love chained

to a rock, then each in the mirror sees
what I see: who I was, became, am now.
Double-locked. Three skylights opened to tease
my menagerie of moths. Some huge, some slow,

too slow for me. Their wingbeat for my heartbeat.
Lying open to the weather, on heat.

Lying open to the weather, on heat,
on Hackney Downs, accompanied by Dante
and Love, his 'gaze on the ground', with *La Vita
Nuova* blurred by sky, I'm near where we lay

that once . . . but you wilt. Sigh. Abbreviate
my name, short as it is, hitch up your glasses,
rub your eyes, gaze into space as if fate
had called from a long way off and impasses

were all you had to go by. Love, so at ease
with bluffs, why don't you revisit a side road,
from a whole lawn pick one of poetry's
old standbys: dandelion clocks I showed you

how to tell time by. Blow. There's still a half-puff
on hold. And I was never one for half.

On hold. And I was never one for half-
etched outlines, loose holds on reality,
but with wingtips skimming grass and its rough
nap pricking shins, wind in my hair, with every

circle they describe, head-high, birds go through me.
Weave passages through flesh and blood, a rush
and throb of beat and swoop, a brush to groom me.
Groom me for vanishing in the clear plush

of air, flesh and fell, absorbed by the sheer
drive of it. And I, my own drives on hold,
who thought I could always steer on course, veer,
take leave of my senses, give in. To cold

winds from your halfway, your 'when-can-we-meet?' –
way, houses. Never did learn to compete.

. . . way houses. Never did learn to compete . . .
might be a fragment unscrabbled from sand,
torn and stained, heeled in from untrammelled feet,
from a stone where an ode, elastic band

were once balled around it; a message sea
spewed, a bad dog chewed and salt or saliva
made the first word run, the last bleed and me
mad about it. For I'm no deepsea diver

to fish unfathomable meanings nor
a mermaid wed to their beds where old seadogs
get wrecked, snore an eternity and more
and she too dumb to kick them, stick those hogs,

make no bones about it. I just get tough
with mild-mannered sisters, cope with rebuff.

With mild-mannered sisters, cope with rebuff,
With sweet serenity, keep your mouth shut
And when charity moans 'nothing's enough
For love, true love', give up those fags, you slut.

Called you a slut once, remember? Of course
you do. Wouldn't even bother to answer
the question. So why is it such a source
of embarrassment to me, yours? Mine never

was to you, was it? Of course it was? Oh.
Forcing me to kiss with a mouth rinsed out
with ashes, was that lust? Hardly think so.
Don't like to think what that was all about.

Thought I'd sing a song. Try it on for size.
Temper quarrels with jokes. Freak storms with sighs . . .

Temper quarrels with jokes. Freak storms with sighs.
That's no song. That's a dirge, mirthless and dour,
'defeated' you'd prefer. And I, loath to rise
to the bait of your defeat being ours,

ours mine, would give nothing away. No use
crying 'when's my turn to be given to,
given to first?' when someone who'll refuse
you nothing, nothing spare, is driven to

give in the ways he can, and can't, and won't
deny he's failed. I wish you had. Wish I
had allowed you to, asked for less, said 'don't
feel that way'. But you did. I didn't. Why

bolt the stable door? Feed self-pity? Covet,
like small rain when drought's at the door, false comfort?

Like small rain when drought's at the door, false comfort
pocks my sleep and I ache, dowsed with the feel
of you, you and you and you, to stay anchored,
moored to black rivers, grounded on the keel

of dream rows unresolved. Dream men, you motley
crew, shape-shifters who slip the hold of nightmare,
shiver in a shaft of motes, ghosts, I'll shortly
have you. But daylight brooks no see-through nightwear,

limbs in limbo. Daylight melts you. Like smells
you could swear you've scrubbed of all trace and can't
understand why they're still in your face, bells
that keep ringing after they've stopped, you'll rant

and rave, finally cave in. Dumb disguise
to borrow heat from the sun when sun lies.

To borrow heat from the sun when sun lies
in your voice, spring from the air when larks sing
at your approach, blush from a peach when fruitflies
buzz as you unload, shyly, everything

money could buy, I'd like, you'll cook, and one
wholenut bar I'd wish were bigger if only
I were smaller, is to belie the sun,
moon, flowers, trees, birds and bees, ads for lonely

hearts I read, secretly, and you don't. Don't
make me do all the wrong things now, like long
to love you. Don't turn my views back to front,
undo my vows, break my heart; leave it strong

enough for being, when sun's desperate
under leaf, heat under cold, 'temperate'.

Under leaf, heat – under cold, 'temperate'
skies now intemperate and glowering
with storms – takes the last of the sun, irate
with gnats, mosquitoes, chainsaws. Flowering

ramblers wilt on walls. England is at peace.
Your country, tiny island, devastated.
Mine, no news. Darling, we are refugees
from love, nurture, nature. And implicated

is our own, so unable to sustain
what is alien, intractable, fuse
colours of a flag into alltime rainbows.
Why not raise the white then? Let's call a truce.

Hand out blessings. Play archbishops and popes.
Let's call it, for it cuts both ways, this trope.

Let's call it, for it cuts both ways, this trope,
this bluff, this marriage of true minds, sly two-way
mirror, bending-the-truth-twice telescope.
Star to ships that pass in the night, a blue bay

that sparkles, green havens, earth's heavens, scrub
them all out, redraw, rewrite them. But this time,
each to his own, don't share them. Only trouble
is, won't they look the same, find the same rhyme

for thee and thine, rivers of wine and maidens'
veils so fine you can see not only limbs move
but marrow through them? For how many heavens
make one, which is the one on earth but love?

And love's not one to – oh grope for it, grope –
to prove even a full sun brings false hope.

To prove even a full sun brings false hope
how many times, when it blazed, did we cling
to shade, pronounce its grey, slippery slope
as safe and flames, homespun, poor candled things

the merest breath can snuff, as passions breath
inflames. Hatred, revulsion, rage. How many
flares did we scorn, each spark a shibboleth?
Prove me wrong. Show me an ear of corn, any

golden thing that grows, any vine tomato
religiously watered, courageously
staked on a windowsill and swear that no
fire, no faith inspired it. Outrageously

prove me wrong. This once. But go it alone.
Twice I've gone as far as the High Street phone.

Ghazal

If I said every tear, each sob, each sigh
quietens, stops and all our tears soon dry,
                              who'd argue?

If I said every voice stung to the cry
'What is the point?' doesn't want a reply,
                              who'd argue?

If I said time will tell, heal, steal, fly –
take it, give it, do with it as you're done by,
                              who'd argue?

But if hopelessness did, who would deny
its right to be heard, if hope were to try,
                              who'd argue?

Who'd argue over love? Who'd follow my
example? You, my love? Then who am I
                              to argue?

Don't Ask me, Love, for that First Love

after Faiz Ahmed Faiz

Don't think I haven't changed. Who said
absence makes the heart grow fonder?
Though I watch the sunset redden
every day, days don't grow longer.

There are many kinds of silence,
none more radiant than the sun's.
Sun is silent in our presence,
unlike love, silent when it's gone.

I thought that every spring was you,
every blossom, every bud;
that summer had little to do
but follow, singing in my blood.

How wrong I was. What had summer
to do with sorrow in full spate?
Every rosebush, every flower
I passed, stood at a stranger's gate.

Weaving through our towns, centuries
of raw silk, brocade and velvet
have swilled the streets in blood. Bodies,
ripe with sores in lanes and markets,

are paying with their lives. But I
had little time for the world's wars,
love was war enough. In your sky,
your eyes, were all my falling stars.

Don't ask me, though I wish you would
and I know you won't, for more tears.
Why build a dam at Sefid Rud
if not to water land for years?

Though we'll never see the olives,
ricefields, shelter in an alcove
from the sun, in our time, our lives
have more to answer to than love.